~A BINGO BOOK~

Oklahoma Bingo Book

COMPLETE BINGO GAME IN A BOOK

OKLAHOMA

Written By Rebecca Stark

ISBN 978-0-87386-529-6

Educational Books 'n' Bingo

Printed in the U.S.A.

DIRECTIONS

INCLUDED:

List of Terms

Templates for Additional Terms and Clues

2 Clues per Term

30 Unique Bingo Cards

Markers

1. **Either cut apart the book or make copies of ALL the sheets. You might want to make an extra copy of the clue sheets to use for introduction and review. Keep the sheets in an envelope for easy reuse.**

2. Cut apart the call cards with terms and clues.

3. Pass out one bingo card per student. There are enough for a class of 30.

4. Pass out markers. You may cut apart the markers included in this book or use any other small items of your choice.

5. Decide whether or not you will require the entire card to be filled. Requiring the entire card to be filled provides a better review. However, if you have a short time to fill, you may prefer to have them do the just the border or some other format. Tell the class before you begin what is required.

6. There are 50 terms. Read the list before you begin. If there are any terms that have not been covered in class, you may want to read to the students the term and clues before you begin.

7. There is a blank space in the middle of each card. You can instruct the students to use it as a free space or you can write in answers to cover terms not included. Of course, in this case you would create your own clues. (Templates provided.)

8. Shuffle the cards and place them in a pile. Two or three clues are provided for each term. If you plan to play the game with the same group more than once, you might want to choose a different clue for each game. If not, you may choose to use more than one clue.

9. Be sure to keep the cards you have used for the present game in a separate pile. When a student calls, "Bingo," he or she will have to verify that the correct answers are on his or her card AND that the markers were placed in response to the proper questions. Pull out the cards that are on the student's card keeping them in the order they were used in the game. Read each clue as it was given and ask the student to identify the correct answer from his or her card.

10. If the student has the correct answers on the card AND has shown that they were marked in response to the *correct questions,* then that student is the winner and the game is over. If the student does not have the correct answers on the card OR he or she marked the answers in response to *the wrong questions,* then the game continues until there is a proper winner.

11. If you want to play again, reshuffle the cards and begin again.

Have fun!

TERMS INCLUDED

Barite Rose	Livestock
Black Mesa	Louisiana Purchase
Border	Mickey Mantle
Buffalo	Mined
Bullfrog	Motto
Cherokee	Musical Instrument
Climate	Norman
Collared Lizard	Oklahoma City
County (-ies)	Oklahoma Territory
Crop(s)	Prairie Plains
Dust Bowl	Raccoon
Executive Branch	Red Beds Plains
Flag	Red River Valley
Flower(s)	Redbud
Guthrie	River(s)
High Plains	Will Rogers
Homestead Act	Saurophaganax Maximus
Honeybee	Scissor-tailed Flycatcher
Hourglass Selenite	Seal
"Howdy Folks"	Song(s)
Industries	Sooners
Judicial Branch	Trail of Tears
Lake(s)	Tulsa
Land Regions	Union
Legislative Branch	White-tailed Deer

Oklahoma Bingo

© Barbara M. Peller

Additional Terms

Choose as many additional terms as you would like and write them in the squares. Repeat each as desired.
Cut out the squares and randomly distribute them to the class.
Instruct the students to place their square on the center space of their card.

Oklahoma Bingo

Clues for Additional Terms

Write three clues for each of your additional terms.

_____ 1. 2. 3.	_____ 1. 2. 3.
_____ 1. 2. 3.	_____ 1. 2. 3.
_____ 1. 2. 3.	_____ 1. 2. 3.

Barite Rose 1. The ___, or rose rock, is the official state rock. 2. ___ rocks are found in only a few places in the world. They are found in clusters. Some clusters weigh hundreds of pounds.	**Black Mesa** 1. At 4,973 feet, ___ is the highest point in the state. 2. ___, the highest point in Oklahoma, is in the western part of the High Plains.
Border 1. Colorado, Kansas, Texas, Missouri, Arkansas, New Mexico, and Texas ___ Oklahoma. 2. The Red River forms the border between Texas and Oklahoma.	**Buffalo** 1. The American ___, or bison, is the state animal. 2. Millions of ___ once roamed the American prairie, providing a way of life for the Plains Indians.
Bullfrog 1. The ___ is the state amphibian. 2. The ___ is the largest frog in North America and can be found throughout the state.	**Cherokee** 1.The ___ Nation has more than 300,000 members; it is the largest of the 565 federally recognized Native American tribes in the United States. 2. Before the "Trail of Tears," the ___ lived in the Southeast. Now their headquarters are in Tahlequah, Oklahoma.
Climate 1. Most of Oklahoma has a warm, dry ___ with generally mild winters. Winter temperatures are highest in the south and steadily decrease to the north. 2. Warm, moist air from the Gulf of Mexico influences the state's ___, especially over the southern and eastern portions of the state.	**Collared Lizard** 1. The ___ is the state reptile. 2. The ___ is also called mountain boomer.
County (-ies) 1. Oklahoma has 77 ___. 2. Oklahoma City is in Oklahoma ___ in the central part of the state.	**Crop(s)** 1. Wheat is Oklahoma's most valuable ___. 2. Wheat, greenhouse and nursery products, hay, soybeans, peanuts, and cotton are among the top cash ___ in the state.

Oklahoma Bingo

Dust Bowl

1. The ___ refers to the area affected by the severe dust storms of the 1930s.
2. In the 1930s tons of topsoil were blown off barren fields and carried in storm clouds for hundreds of miles. The driest region of the Plains, which included the Oklahoma Panhandle, became known as the ___.

Executive Branch

1. The governor, lt. governor, attorney general, district attorney, and secretary of state are all part of the ___ of government.
2. The governor is the chief officer of the ___. The present-day ___ is [fill in].

Flag

1. The state ___ depicts an Osage warrior's shield centered on a field of blue.
2. Over the shield on the state ___ are the symbols of peace and unity for both Native American and European-American cultures: the calumet, or ceremonial peace pipe, and the olive branch.

Flower(s)

1. Three ___ are official state symbols: the Oklahoma rose, Indian blanket, and mistletoe.
2. Indian Blanket, the official wild___, is also called firewheel.

Guthrie

1. ___ was the first capital of Oklahoma.
2. The state capital was moved from ___ to Oklahoma City in 1910.

High Plains

1. The ___ is a region of flat grasslands; they spread across northwestern Oklahoma and include the Panhandle.
2. The ___ are part of the Great Plains of North America. The region is called the ___ because the land rises as high as 2,000 feet on the eastern edge to 4,973 feet at Black Mesa, the highest point in the state.

Homestead Act

1. Under the terms of the ___ of 1862, a person could get 160 acres of free land by living on and improving the land for 5 years.
2. Under the terms of the ___, anyone 21 or older who had never taken up arms against the U.S. government, including freed slaves, could file an application to claim a federal land grant.

Honeybee

1. The ___ is the state insect.
2. The ___ is an official state symbol in 17 states, probably because the insect plays such an important role in agriculture.

Hourglass Selenite

1. ___ is the state crystal.
2. ___ crystals are found only on the salt plains of Oklahoma.

"Howdy Folks"

1. ___, by David Randolph Milsten, is the state poem.
2. ___, the state poem, was the official poem of Will Rogers.

Oklahoma Bingo

Industries 1. Farming, oil, and natural gas are major ___ in the state. 2. Oil refining, meat packing, food processing, and the manufacture of machinery—especially construction and oil equipment—are important ___.	**Judicial Branch** 1. The ___ of government interprets the laws. The Oklahoma Court System comprises the Supreme Court, the Court of Criminal Appeals, the Court of Civil Appeals, and 77 District Courts. 2. Unlike the ___ of most states, Oklahoma has 2 courts of last resort: the Supreme Court and the Court of Criminal Appeals.
Lake(s) 1. Oklahoma has more than 200 ___ that were created by dams; that is more than any other state. 2. Broken Bow ___ is located in southeastern Oklahoma in the Kiamichi Mountains. It has 180 miles of shoreline.	**Land Regions** 1. Oklahoma's landscape includes flat, fertile plains and low hills. There are 10 distinct ___. 2. The 10 ___ are the Ozark Plateau, the Prairie Plains, the Ouachita Mountains, the Sandstone Hills, the Arbuckle Mountains, the Wichita Mountains, the Red River Valley Region, the Red Beds Plains, the Gypsum Hills, and the High Plains.
Legislative Branch 1. The ___ of government comprises the Senate and the House of Representatives. 2. The ___ of government makes the laws.	**Livestock** 1. ___ products account for more than half of Oklahoma's annual farm receipts. They include cattle, dairy products, swine, and broilers. 2. Beef cattle is the most important ___ product and the leading source of agricultural income in the state.
Louisiana Purchase 1. The United States acquired most of Oklahoma in 1803 as a result of the ___. 2. The Oklahoma Panhandle was not included in the ___. It did not become U.S. territory until the annexation of Texas in 1845.	**Mickey Mantle** 1. This hall-of-fame baseball player was born in Spavinaw, Oklahoma, and grew up in Commerce. 2. His childhood home and the old tin barn where he practiced still stand in Commerce.
Mined 1. Oil ,natural gas, crushed stone, iodine, and sand and gravel are important ___ products. Iodine is not produced in any other state. 2. Oil and natural gas are by far the most important ___ products.	**Motto** 1. The state ___ is *"Labor omnia vincit."* It dates back over 2,000 years to the writing of a Roman poet named Virgil. 2. The English translation of the state ___ is "Labor conquers all things."

Oklahoma Bingo

Musical Instrument 1. The fiddle is the official state ___. 2. The drum is the state percussive ___.	**Norman** 1. ___ is the third largest city in the state. The main campus of the University of Oklahoma is here. 2. The National Weather Center is located on the campus of the University of Oklahoma in ___.
Oklahoma City 1. ___ is the capital and largest city in Oklahoma. 2. The National Cowboy and Western Heritage Museum and the Oklahoma History Center are both in ___.	**Oklahoma Territory** 1. The area set aside as Indian Territory in 1834 was divided into Indian Territory and ___ on May 2, 1890. 2. Indian Territory and ___ were combined to create the state of Oklahoma, on November 16, 1907.
Prairie Plains 1. The ___ are between the Ozark Plateau and the Sandstone Hills. Most of the state's coal and much of its oil is produced in this region. 2. The ___ area lies west and south of the Ozark Plateau. Farming and cattle ranching take place there.	**Raccoon** 1. This mammal is the official state furbearer, meaning that it was traditionally hunted and trapped primarily for fur. 2. The name of this mammal is derived from the Algonquian Indian word *"aroughcoune,"* which means "he who scratches with his hands."
Red Beds Plains 1. The ___ is the largest land region in the state. It starts at the Kansas border in the north and continues south through the center of the state. 2. The eastern part of this large land region has some forested areas. The western part is covered with grass.	**Red River Region** 1. The ___ Region is in southern Oklahoma along the Texas border. It is characterized by rolling prairie and forests. 2. The soil of the ___ in southern Oklahoma is sandy and fertile. Cotton, peanuts, and a variety of vegetables are grown in this region.
Redbud 1. The ___ is the state tree. 2. The reddish-pink blossoms of this small, deciduous tree brighten the landscape throughout the state before others have even produced leaves.	**River(s)** 1. The Arkansas, Canadian, and Red are ___ in Oklahoma. 2. The Arkansas ___ is a major tributary of the Mississippi.

Will Rogers 1. This cowboy, entertainer, humorist, and social commentator was one of the world's best-known celebrities of the 1920s and 1930s. 2. "Howdy Folks," the state poem, is his official poem. This Oklahoman entertainer and humorist is in the National Cowboy Hall of Fame.	**Saurophaganax Maximus** 1. ____ is the state official state fossil. 2. ____, the state fossil, was found in Oklahoma. It has been called the greatest predator of earth's history.
Scissor-tailed Flycatcher 1. The ____ is the state bird and is depicted on the state quarter. 2. This bird is of great economic value because its diet consists almost entirely of non-useful and harmful insects.	**Seal** 1. The Great ____ depicts the official seals of the Chickasaw Nation, the Cherokee Nation, the Choctaw Nation, the Creek Nation, and the Seminole Nation. 2. The 45 small stars on the Great ____ represent the other 45 states. The large center star symbolizes Oklahoma. Its 5 radiating arms represent each of the 5 Civilized Indian Nations.
Song(s) 1. Oklahoma has several state ____. The official state ____ and anthem is "Oklahoma!" It was written by Rogers and Hammerstein. 2. The official children's ____ is "Oklahoma, My Native Land."	**Sooners** 1. Those who entered the Unassigned Lands in what is now Oklahoma before President Cleveland proclaimed them open to settlement were called ____. 2. Sometimes Oklahomans are called ____.
Trail of Tears 1. The Cherokee people referred to their forced migration as the ____. 2. The forced relocation of Native Americans from the Southeast following the Indian Removal Act of 1830 was called the ____ by the Cherokee.	**Tulsa** 1. ____ is the second largest city in the state. The Philbrook and Gilcrease museums are in this city. 2. ____ is situated on the Arkansas River at the foothills of the Ozark Mountains in northeast Oklahoma.
Union 1. Oklahoma entered the ____ on November 16, 1907, as the 46th state. 2. Oklahoma and the Indian Territories entered the ____ together as one state.	**White-tailed Deer** 1. The ____ is the state game mammal. 2. ____ are able to run up to 40 miles per hour, jump 9-foot fences, and swim at 13 miles per hour. The white underside of its tail waves when running and is flashed to signal danger.
Oklahoma Bingo	© Barbara M. Peller

Oklahoma Bingo

Red River Valley	Barite Rose	Border	Hourglass Selenite	Bullfrog
Homestead Act	Black Mesa	Tulsa	Musical Instrument	Will Rogers
Trail of Tears	Motto		Prairie Plains	Union
Sooners	River(s)	Song(s)	Mickey Mantle	Mined
Oklahoma Territory	Judicial Branch	Flower(s)	Scissor-tailed Flycatcher	Legislative Branch

Oklahoma Bingo: Card No. 1

Oklahoma Bingo

Sooners	Trail of Tears	Land Regions	Redbud	Louisiana Purchase
Mined	Guthrie	Collared Lizard	River(s)	Oklahoma City
Crop(s)	Judicial Branch		Lake(s)	Song(s)
Raccoon	Red Beds Plains	Motto	White-tailed Deer	Bullfrog
Will Rogers	Tulsa	Flower(s)	Homestead Act	Scissor-tailed Flycatcher

Oklahoma Bingo

Judicial Branch	Song(s)	Guthrie	Mickey Mantle	Trail of Tears
Mined	Black Mesa	County (-ies)	Barite Rose	Industries
River(s)	Tulsa		Oklahoma City	Buffalo
Motto	Crop(s)	Oklahoma Territory	Raccoon	Land Regions
Scissor-tailed Flycatcher	Dust Bowl	Flower(s)	White-tailed Deer	Louisiana Purchase

Oklahoma Bingo: Card No. 3

Oklahoma Bingo

Motto	Oklahoma City	Border	Dust Bowl	Louisiana Purchase
Norman	Climate	Barite Rose	Redbud	Trail of Tears
Prairie Plains	Raccoon		Legislative Branch	Hourglass Selenite
Song(s)	Black Mesa	Tulsa	Flower(s)	Collared Lizard
Executive Branch	Will Rogers	Cherokee	Scissor-tailed Flycatcher	Union

Oklahoma Bingo: Card No. 4

Oklahoma Bingo

Will Rogers	Bullfrog	River(s)	Collared Lizard	Dust Bowl
Norman	Song(s)	County (-ies)	Lake(s)	Black Mesa
Border	Union		Musical Instrument	"Howdy Folks"
Legislative Branch	Louisiana Purchase	Red River Valley	White-tailed Deer	Flag
Guthrie	Flower(s)	Trail of Tears	Motto	Prairie Plains

Oklahoma Bingo: Card No. 5

Oklahoma Bingo

Buffalo	Oklahoma City	Land Regions	Louisiana Purchase	Union
Mickey Mantle	River(s)	Flag	Barite Rose	Trail of Tears
Redbud	Executive Branch		Climate	Lake(s)
Flower(s)	Oklahoma Territory	White-tailed Deer	Cherokee	Border
Mined	Collared Lizard	Red River Valley	Prairie Plains	High Plains

Oklahoma Bingo: Card No. 6

Oklahoma Bingo

Red River Valley	Oklahoma City	"Howdy Folks"	Song(s)	Guthrie
Mined	Louisiana Purchase	Judicial Branch	Black Mesa	Norman
Union	Hourglass Selenite		Lake(s)	Climate
Motto	Raccoon	County (-ies)	Sooners	Crop(s)
Flower(s)	Dust Bowl	White-tailed Deer	Cherokee	Buffalo

Oklahoma Bingo: Card No. 7

Oklahoma Bingo

Prairie Plains	Oklahoma City	Honeybee	Mickey Mantle	Climate
Norman	Border	Redbud	Union	Collared Lizard
High Plains	Dust Bowl		Louisiana Purchase	Bullfrog
Scissor-tailed Flycatcher	Motto	Sooners	Executive Branch	Raccoon
Tulsa	Flower(s)	Cherokee	River(s)	Mined

Oklahoma Bingo

Lake(s)	Guthrie	Judicial Branch	High Plains	Dust Bowl
Executive Branch	Louisiana Purchase	Prairie Plains	River(s)	Oklahoma City
Industries	Red River Valley		Black Mesa	Honeybee
Flag	Bullfrog	Oklahoma Territory	Musical Instrument	"Howdy Folks"
Raccoon	White-tailed Deer	County (-ies)	Sooners	Legislative Branch

Oklahoma Bingo: Card No. 9

Oklahoma Bingo

Sooners	Mickey Mantle	Climate	Redbud	High Plains
Union	Collared Lizard	Barite Rose	Black Mesa	Louisiana Purchase
Dust Bowl	Oklahoma City		Hourglass Selenite	Crop(s)
Oklahoma Territory	Legislative Branch	Flag	White-tailed Deer	Industries
County (-ies)	Mined	Land Regions	Will Rogers	Prairie Plains

Oklahoma Bingo: Card No. 10

© Barbara M. Peller

Oklahoma Bingo

Buffalo	Oklahoma City	River(s)	Flag	Mined
Honeybee	Industries	Musical Instrument	Lake(s)	Barite Rose
Norman	Louisiana Purchase		Land Regions	Judicial Branch
County (-ies)	Trail of Tears	White-tailed Deer	Dust Bowl	Sooners
Executive Branch	Flower(s)	Red River Valley	Cherokee	Guthrie

Oklahoma Bingo: Card No. 11

Oklahoma Bingo

Guthrie	Bullfrog	Industries	Mickey Mantle	Lake(s)
Judicial Branch	Mined	Border	Cherokee	Black Mesa
Red River Valley	"Howdy Folks"		Union	Redbud
Flower(s)	Raccoon	Louisiana Purchase	Sooners	Norman
Oklahoma City	Honeybee	Dust Bowl	Executive Branch	Collared Lizard

Oklahoma Bingo: Card No. 12

Oklahoma Bingo

Flag	Bullfrog	Buffalo	Industries	Union
Border	Honeybee	Louisiana Purchase	Lake(s)	Crop(s)
Mickey Mantle	Collared Lizard		Judicial Branch	"Howdy Folks"
Prairie Plains	White-tailed Deer	Climate	Dust Bowl	Sooners
Flower(s)	Legislative Branch	Cherokee	Red River Valley	Musical Instrument

Oklahoma Bingo: Card No. 13

Oklahoma Bingo

Homestead Act	Louisiana Purchase	River(s)	Lake(s)	Executive Branch
Collared Lizard	Red River Valley	Industries	Black Mesa	Oklahoma City
Flag	Hourglass Selenite		Land Regions	County (-ies)
Legislative Branch	White-tailed Deer	Dust Bowl	Climate	Buffalo
Flower(s)	Redbud	Crop(s)	Mined	Prairie Plains

Oklahoma Bingo

Musical Instrument	Lake(s)	River(s)	Guthrie	Mickey Mantle
Buffalo	Land Regions	Barite Rose	Border	Executive Branch
Union	Red River Valley		Trail of Tears	Oklahoma City
Flower(s)	Industries	Honeybee	White-tailed Deer	Flag
Mined	Raccoon	Cherokee	High Plains	Judicial Branch

Oklahoma Bingo: Card No. 15

Oklahoma Bingo

Climate	Industries	Honeybee	High Plains	Red Beds Plains
Redbud	Crop(s)	"Howdy Folks"	Norman	Hourglass Selenite
Flag	Bullfrog		Union	Judicial Branch
Motto	Collared Lizard	Flower(s)	Musical Instrument	Sooners
Executive Branch	Seal	Cherokee	Raccoon	Oklahoma City

Oklahoma Bingo: Card No. 16

Oklahoma Bingo

County (-ies)	*Saurophagana x Maximus*	Livestock	Industries	Homestead Act
Musical Instrument	Executive Branch	White-tailed Deer	Hourglass Selenite	"Howdy Folks"
Lake(s)	Prairie Plains		Seal	Honeybee
Legislative Branch	Mined	Sooners	River(s)	Crop(s)
Oklahoma Territory	Flag	Guthrie	Mickey Mantle	Bullfrog

Oklahoma Bingo

High Plains	Dust Bowl	Collared Lizard	Flag	Redbud
Oklahoma City	County (-ies)	Oklahoma Territory	Union	Executive Branch
Lake(s)	Crop(s)		Livestock	Border
Bullfrog	Barite Rose	White-tailed Deer	Sooners	Land Regions
Seal	Industries	River(s)	*Saurophagana x Maximus*	Buffalo

Oklahoma Bingo: Card No. 18

Oklahoma Bingo

Union	Buffalo	Industries	Honeybee	Sooners
Musical Instrument	Mickey Mantle	Oklahoma City	Guthrie	Hourglass Selenite
Saurophagana x Maximus	Dust Bowl		Black Mesa	Trail of Tears
Land Regions	Seal	Oklahoma Territory	Raccoon	Livestock
Border	Red Beds Plains	Mined	Prairie Plains	Cherokee

Oklahoma Bingo

Homestead Act	*Saurophagana x Maximus*	Mickey Mantle	Industries	Cherokee
Collared Lizard	Judicial Branch	Norman	Oklahoma Territory	Redbud
Bullfrog	"Howdy Folks"		Motto	Barite Rose
Will Rogers	Tulsa	Scissor-tailed Flycatcher	Raccoon	Seal
Song(s)	Prairie Plains	Red Beds Plains	Sooners	Livestock

Oklahoma Bingo: Card No. 20

Oklahoma Bingo

Musical Instrument	Buffalo	Norman	Industries	Will Rogers
Bullfrog	Livestock	Climate	Honeybee	Red River Valley
Crop(s)	Mined		*Saurophagana x Maximus*	River(s)
Oklahoma Territory	Guthrie	Seal	Legislative Branch	Prairie Plains
Motto	Red Beds Plains	Cherokee	County (-ies)	Raccoon

Oklahoma Bingo

High Plains	Land Regions	Livestock	Border	Flag
Redbud	Mickey Mantle	Trail of Tears	Honeybee	Black Mesa
Collared Lizard	Hourglass Selenite		Red River Valley	"Howdy Folks"
Seal	Legislative Branch	Raccoon	Barite Rose	Norman
Red Beds Plains	County (-ies)	*Saurophagana x Maximus*	Crop(s)	Motto

Oklahoma Bingo: Card No. 22

Oklahoma Bingo

Climate	*Saurophagana x Maximus*	Guthrie	Border	Cherokee
Buffalo	Homestead Act	Mined	Musical Instrument	Barite Rose
Land Regions	Flag		Scissor-tailed Flycatcher	Red River Valley
Crop(s)	Red Beds Plains	Seal	County (-ies)	Raccoon
Will Rogers	Tulsa	Prairie Plains	Oklahoma Territory	Livestock

Oklahoma Bingo: Card No. 23

Oklahoma Bingo

Climate	Prairie Plains	Homestead Act	*Saurophagana x Maximus*	Honeybee
Livestock	Cherokee	Norman	Redbud	Red River Valley
"Howdy Folks"	High Plains		Flag	Crop(s)
Will Rogers	Scissor-tailed Flycatcher	Seal	County (-ies)	Bullfrog
Song(s)	Motto	Red Beds Plains	Mickey Mantle	Tulsa

Oklahoma Bingo

Motto	Norman	*Saurophagana x Maximus*	River(s)	Livestock
Barite Rose	Bullfrog	Musical Instrument	Climate	Black Mesa
Legislative Branch	Honeybee		Scissor-tailed Flycatcher	Seal
Trail of Tears	Will Rogers	Tulsa	Red Beds Plains	Hourglass Selenite
Cherokee	Homestead Act	Collared Lizard	Executive Branch	Song(s)

Oklahoma Bingo: Card No. 25

Oklahoma Bingo

Livestock	*Saurophagana x Maximus*	Land Regions	Redbud	High Plains
Oklahoma Territory	Mickey Mantle	Honeybee	Homestead Act	Climate
Legislative Branch	Scissor-tailed Flycatcher		Hourglass Selenite	Motto
County (-ies)	Border	Will Rogers	Red Beds Plains	Seal
"Howdy Folks"	Executive Branch	River(s)	Tulsa	Song(s)

Oklahoma Bingo: Card No. 26

Oklahoma Bingo

Land Regions	Collared Lizard	*Saurophagana x Maximus*	Homestead Act	Judicial Branch
Will Rogers	Scissor-tailed Flycatcher	Musical Instrument	Seal	Black Mesa
White-tailed Deer	Tulsa		Red Beds Plains	Motto
High Plains	Buffalo	Norman	Song(s)	Barite Rose
Executive Branch	Hourglass Selenite	Livestock	Trail of Tears	"Howdy Folks"

Oklahoma Bingo: Card No. 27

Oklahoma Bingo

Land Regions	Homestead Act	Trail of Tears	*Saurophagana x Maximus*	Climate
Judicial Branch	Livestock	Scissor-tailed Flycatcher	Redbud	Hourglass Selenite
Tulsa	Crop(s)		"Howdy Folks"	Oklahoma Territory
Sooners	High Plains	Mined	Red Beds Plains	Seal
Border	Lake(s)	Executive Branch	Song(s)	Will Rogers

Oklahoma Bingo

Livestock	Homestead Act	High Plains	Musical Instrument	Lake(s)
Raccoon	Oklahoma Territory	Norman	"Howdy Folks"	Trail of Tears
Legislative Branch	Scissor-tailed Flycatcher		Black Mesa	*Saurophagana x Maximus*
Judicial Branch	Will Rogers	Louisiana Purchase	Red Beds Plains	Seal
Climate	Honeybee	Song(s)	Buffalo	Tulsa

Oklahoma Bingo

Dust Bowl	*Saurophagana x Maximus*	Redbud	Lake(s)	Seal
Barite Rose	Homestead Act	Land Regions	Hourglass Selenite	Black Mesa
Legislative Branch	Flag		"Howdy Folks"	Norman
Song(s)	Buffalo	Border	Red Beds Plains	Scissor-tailed Flycatcher
Will Rogers	Union	Tulsa	Livestock	Trail of Tears